ABOUT MAGIC READERS

ABDO continues its commitment to quality books with the nonfiction Magic Readers series. This series includes three levels of books to help students progress to being independent readers while learning factual information. Different levels are intended to reflect the stages of reading in the early grades, helping to select the best level for each individual student.

Level 1: Books with short sentences and familiar words or patterns to share with children who are beginning to understand how letters and sounds go together.

Level 2: Books with longer words and sentences and more complex language patterns with less repetition for progressing readers who are practicing common words and letter sounds.

Level 3: Books with more developed language and vocabulary for transitional readers who are using strategies to figure out unknown words and are ready to learn information more independently.

These nonfiction readers are aligned with the Common Core State Standards progression of literacy, following the sequence of skills and increasing the difficulty of language while engaging the curious minds of young children. These books also reflect the increasing importance of reading informational material in the early grades. They encourage children to read for fun and to learn!

Hannah E. Tolles, MA Reading Specialist

www.abdopublishing.com

Published by Magic Wagon, a division of ABDO, PO Box 398166, Minneapolis, Minnesota 55439. Copyright © 2015 by Abdo Consulting Group, Inc. International copyrights reserved in all countries. No part of this book may be reproduced in any form without written permission from the publisher. Magic Readers™ is a trademark and logo of Magic Wagon.

Printed in the United States of America, North Mankato, Minnesota.
062014
092014

THIS BOOK CONTAINS
RECYCLED MATERIALS

Cover Photo: Thinkstock
Interior Photos: Getty Images, iStockphoto, Shutterstock, Thinkstock

Written and edited by Rochelle Baltzer, Heidi M. D. Elston,
   Megan M. Gunderson, and Bridget O'Brien
Illustrated by Candice Keimig
Designed by Candice Keimig and Jillian O'Brien

Library of Congress Cataloging-in-Publication Data

O'Brien, Bridget, 1991- author.
  Alligators in the swamp / written and edited by Bridget O'Brien [and three others] ; designed and illustrated by Candice Keimig.
    pages cm. -- (Magic readers. Level 3)
  Audience: Ages 5-8.
  ISBN 978-1-62402-056-8
  1. Alligators--Juvenile literature. I. Keimig, Candice, illustrator. II. Title.
  QL666.C925O276 2015
  597.98'4--dc23
                  2014016130

Magic Readers

level
3

Alligators
in the Swamp

By Bridget O'Brien
Illustrated photos by Candice Keimig

Magic Readers

An Imprint of Magic Wagon
www.abdopublishing.com

Alligators have been around for millions of years.

They lived at the same time as dinosaurs!

Today, American alligators are the largest reptiles in North America.

They are the state reptile of Florida.

Alligators live in the southeastern United States.

They live in swamps. They also live in freshwater lakes and streams.

Alligators spend time on land.
They lie in the sun to stay warm.

But, alligators spend most of
their time in the water. They can
hold their breath for 45 minutes!

An alligator can swim, walk,
run, and crawl.

It can lift its heavy tail while it walks.

An alligator digs a den. It digs with its snout and strong tail.

It stays in the den when it is too hot or too cold outside.

Alligators share their home with birds, snakes, bugs, turtles, and fish.

American alligators are like crocodiles and Chinese alligators.

Crocodile

Chinese Alligator

People often mix up crocodiles
and American alligators.

Crocodile

American Alligator

But, a crocodile has a pointed snout. And, two big teeth show when its mouth is closed!

Chinese alligators are smaller than American alligators.

They live only in China. There are not many left in the wild.

American alligators usually stay
away from people.

Sometimes people hunt them for their meat and their skin.

People like to see alligators on TV, in zoos, and in the wild.